SHENANDOAH

PHILIP ROSE, GLORIA & LOUIS K. SHER
present

SHENANDOAH

starring

JOHN CULLUM

Music by
GARY GELD

Lyrics by
PETER UDELL

Book by
JAMES LEE BARRETT
PETER UDELL & PHILIP ROSE

with

DONNA THEODORE   **PENELOPE MILFORD**

JOEL HIGGINS   TED AGRESS   GORDON HALLIDAY

CHIP FORD   JOSEPH SHAPIRO

ROBERT ROSEN   DAVID RUSSELL   JORDAN SUFFIN
GARY HARGER   CHARLES WELCH   EDWARD PENN   ED PREBLE
CRAIG LUCAS   GENE MASONER   CASPER ROOS   MARSHALL THOMAS

Orchestrations by
DON WALKER

Musical Direction by
LYNN CRIGLER

Dance Arrangements by
RUSSELL WARNER

Scenery by
C. Murawski

Lighting by
Thomas Skelton

Costumes by
Pearl Somner & Winn Morton

Choreography by
ROBERT TUCKER

Directed by
PHILIP ROSE

Based on an Original Screenplay by
James Lee Barrett

Originally Presented by The Goodspeed Opera House
Michael P. Price, Executive Producer

Applications for performance of this work, whether legitimate, stock,
amateur, or foreign, should be addressed to:
SAMUEL FRENCH
45 West 25th Street
New York, NY 10010

ISBN 0-88188-109-0

HAL•LEONARD®
CORPORATION
7777 W. BLUEMOUND RD. P.O. BOX 13819 MILWAUKEE, WI 53213

Visit Hal Leonard Online at
www.halleonard.com

JOHN CULLUM

Left to Right
John Cullum, Joel Higgins, Ted Agress, Donna Theodore, David Russell,
Jordan Suffin, Penelope Milford, Robert Rosen and Joseph Shapiro.

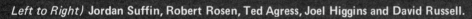

Left to Right) Jordan Suffin, Robert Rosen, Ted Agress, Joel Higgins and David Russell.

Left to Right
Gordon Halliday, Penelope Milford, Robert Rosen, David Russell and Jordan Suffin.

Donna Theodore and Chip Ford

CONTENTS

Cover, Courtesy of RCA Records

RAISE THE FLAG OF DIXIE

Lyric by
PETER UDELL

Music by
GARY GELD

*⬚C = Confederates

⬚U = Union

4

Un - ion boys are hard as nails, John - ny__ Reb - el is a cot - ton - tail.

Well, I'm on my way to __ where they say, "Y' all" and "Hush my

mouth."__ Gon - na raise some hell with a South - ern belle and learn to love the

South. Run 'em down them Stars 'n' Bars. Fly 'em high them Stripes and Stars.

als. C My rib - bons U My med - als C My rib - bons U My

med - als. C My rib - bons! U Med - als! C Rib - bons! U Med - als!
(shouted)

U Moun - tain boy got news for you: Ya

bit off more__ than__ you can chew. C Doo - dle Jim, you soon won't grin when

14

I'VE HEARD IT ALL BEFORE

Lyric by
PETER UDELL

Music by
GARY GELD

"What was the dy-in' for?"_____ The liv-in' can't re-mem-ber,_____ The dead no long-er care._____ But next time it won't hap-pen Up-on my soul I swear._____ I've heard it all, a hun-dred times,

Gm/Eb D11 Ab Tacet

I've heard it all be - fore._____ Don't tell me "It's

ff

Gm F Tacet F Gm Tacet Gm

dif-f'rent now."_____ I've heard it all, I've heard it all,

mp cresc.

F7 Tacet ten. D7-9

I've heard it all be - fore._____

ten. 8va_____ loco

molto rit. f tempo accel.

Gm(maj7)
(add A)

L. H. 8va_____ 15va

8va bassa

WHY AM I ME?

Lyric by
PETER UDELL

Music by
GARY GELD

some - bod - y puts ___ the "who" in - to folks ___ like drop - pin' a stone ___ in a lake. ___

(simile)

So may - be I'm think - in' I'm A - bra-ham Lin - coln and

some - bod - y made ___ a mis - take! If I were

rit.

NEXT TO LOVIN'
(I Like Fightin' Best)

Lyric by
PETER UDELL

Music by
GARY GELD

Bright Country style

1. Jes' cuz I'm for broth-er-hood, Love 'n' peace 'n' moth-er-hood,
2. You just see a gen-tle soul, Hap-py in a pas-sive role,
3. I'm just like a bum-ble-bee, Sip-pin' hon-ey peace-ful-ly,

No one pops the but-tons off my vest.
You don't see a tur-key you can roast.
Heav-en knows I would-n't hurt a fly.

But

I can bust a ma - ple tree clean in half a - cross my knee And I
I can split an eight foot rail with just my lit - tle fin - ger - nail And I
if you poke a - round my hive, you'll be sor - ry you're a - live And I

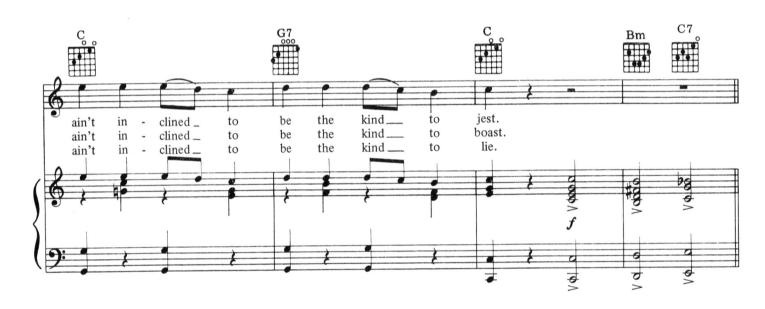

ain't in - clined _ to be the kind _ to jest.
ain't in - clined _ to be the kind _ to boast.
ain't in - clined _ to be the kind _ to lie.

Next to lov - in' I like fight - in', I like fight - in', it's ex - cit - in',
Next to lov - in' I like fight - in', I like fight - in', it's ex - cit - in',
Next to lov - in' I like fight - in', I like fight - in', it's ex - cit - in',

OVER THE HILL

Lyric by
PETER UDELL

Music by
GARY GELD

37

I'm old and gray that I have - n't got more of to give you to -

day? With bats in the at - tic and frost on the sill,

Will - in' or not I'll be o - ver

the hill.

THE PICKERS ARE COMIN'

Lyric by
PETER UDELL

Music by
GARY GELD

MEDITATION I

Lyric by
PETER UDELL

Music by
GARY GELD

54

WE MAKE A BEAUTIFUL PAIR

Lyric by
PETER UDELL

Music by
GARY GELD

60

VIOLETS AND SILVERBELLS

Lyric by
PETER UDELL

Music by
GARY GELD

Vi - 'lets and sil - ver - bells, _____ grapes on the vine. _____

Love, like a vine-yard grows del - i - cate wine. _____

Sug - ar 'n' cin - na - mon, pep - per and spice,___

Love is the re - ci - pe that fla - vors a life.___

Sure as the bri - er and bram - ble en - twine___

So it will al - ways be your dreams and mine.___

poco rall.

IT'S A BOY!

Lyric by
PETER UDELL

Music by
GARY GELD

Tie her a bow of scar - let rib - bon, We got - ta crown a

ti - ny curl. Pick out a ten - der tune for sing - in',

I got - ta wel - come me a

(Shout) girl!

PAPA'S GONNA MAKE IT ALRIGHT

Lyric by
PETER UDELL

Music by
GARY GELD

FREEDOM

Lyric by
PETER UDELL

Music by
GARY GELD

Free - dom, free - dom, Free - dom, free - dom.

Free-dom is a flame that burns with-in ya, Free-dom's in the state____ of mind.

Baa - baa - baa - baa - baa Baa - baa - baa - baa - baa Baa - baa - baa - baa Baa - baa.

Free-dom ain't a boat that's leav-in' with-out ya, Free-dom ain't a place ya

VIOLETS AND SILVERBELLS

(Reprise)

Lyric by
PETER UDELL

Music by
GARY GELD

THE ONLY HOME I KNOW

Lyric by
PETER UDELL

Music by
GARY GELD

87

MEDITATION II

Lyric by
PETER UDELL

Music by
GARY GELD

PASS THE CROSS TO ME

Lyric by
PETER UDELL

Music by
GARY GELD

Let me stray not like a spar-row in a storm.___ Let me cast not to the ground my crown of thorn.___ I will bear it, you can pass the Cross to me.___ Pass the Cross and I will bear it faith-ful-

ly._____ I am read - y,_____ I am read - y,____ I am

read - y, you can pass the Cross to me._____ For to suf - fer as the Lord is to

have my soul re - stored. Let this faith of mine be tried, for the

Lord is by my side. I am read - y,_____ I am read - y,___ I am